100

Great Leaders

Ramses II
[1320 B.C. - 1224 B.C.]

Ramses II the Great was the third king of Egypt's 19th dynasty. Soon after becoming the king, he began a series of wars, the most famous being the Battle of Kadesh. He expanded his empire as far as ancient Ethiopia (now Sudan). Egypt prospered under Ramses II, whose reign was the second longest in Egyptian history. According to legend, he was the pharaoh (Egyptian king) against whom Moses rebelled.

1320 B.C.: *Born to Seti 1 and Queen Tuya*

1290 B.C.: *Becomes pharaoh after his father's death*

1224 B.C.: *Dies at the age of 96*

Ramses II

Cyrus the Great

Cyrus the Great
[c. 599 B.C. - c. 529 B.C.]

Cyrus the Great was king of Persia and the founder of the vast Persian Empire. In 550 B.C., he defeated the Median rulers and conquered Ecbatana. Subsequently, he extended his control to Lydia and Babylon, establishing the Persian Empire as the biggest power in the world. Cyrus was liked by all because of his generosity towards his people.

599 B.C.: *Born to Cambyses, ruler of Anshan*

559 B.C.: *Succeeds his father to the throne*

550 B.C.: *Defeats Astyages, the last of the Median rulers*

546 B.C.: *Becomes the king of Persia and conquers Lydia*

538 B.C.: *Conquers Babylon*

3 Pericles
[495 B.C. - 429 B.C.]

Pericles was one of the greatest democratic leaders of Athens. Under him Athens prospered and became very powerful. He built several monuments, including the Parthenon. The period between 461 and 379 B.C. is also known as the "Age of Pericles". However, the rise of Athens under Pericles was resented by neighbouring kingdoms and that led to the Peloponnesian War. During the war a plague spread through Athens, killing Pericles and most of his family.

495 B.C.: *Born to Xanthippus and Agariste*

458 B.C.: *Elected strategos (general)*

447 B.C.: *Work on the Parthenon starts*

429 B.C.: *Dies*

Pericles

Alexander

4 Demosthenes
[384 B.C. - 322 B.C.]

Known for his inspiring speeches, it is hard to believe that as a child Demosthenes stammered while speaking. The legend goes that Demosthenes, determined to overcome his problem, talked with pebbles in his mouth and recited verses while running! Indeed, by the age of 25 he could speak clearly. His powerful speeches against the invasion of Greece by King Philip of Macedonia, are famous.

384 B.C.: *Born to a rich sword maker in Athens*

377 B.C.: *Orphaned at the tender age of seven*

330 B.C.: *Gives his greatest oration, "On the Crown"*

322 B.C.: *Swallows poison after failing in his efforts to free Greece from Macedonia*

5 Alexander the Great
[356 B.C. - 323 B.C.]

356 B.C.: *Born in Pella, to King Philip II of Macedonia*

336 B.C.: *Becomes king after Philip II is killed*

333 B.C.: *Defeats Darius III in the Battle of Issus*

332 B.C.: *Reaches Egypt, where he is accepted as the pharaoh; founds a city, later named Alexandria after him*

July 331 B.C. *Defeats Darius again; becomes the "king of Asia"*

327 B.C.: *Defeats King Porus*

June 13, 323 B.C.: *Dies in Babylon*

Alexander the Great was the king of Macedonia. He conquered most of the world, including the powerful Persian Empire. His victory against Darius III, king of Persia, won him the title, "king of Asia". Marching towards India, Alexander defeated King Porus at Hydaspes River (now Jhelum). Not satisfied, Alexander continued on his mission until his soldiers refused to go further. He, too, had grown weak from his wounds and long battles and died unable to fulfil his dream of conquering the world.

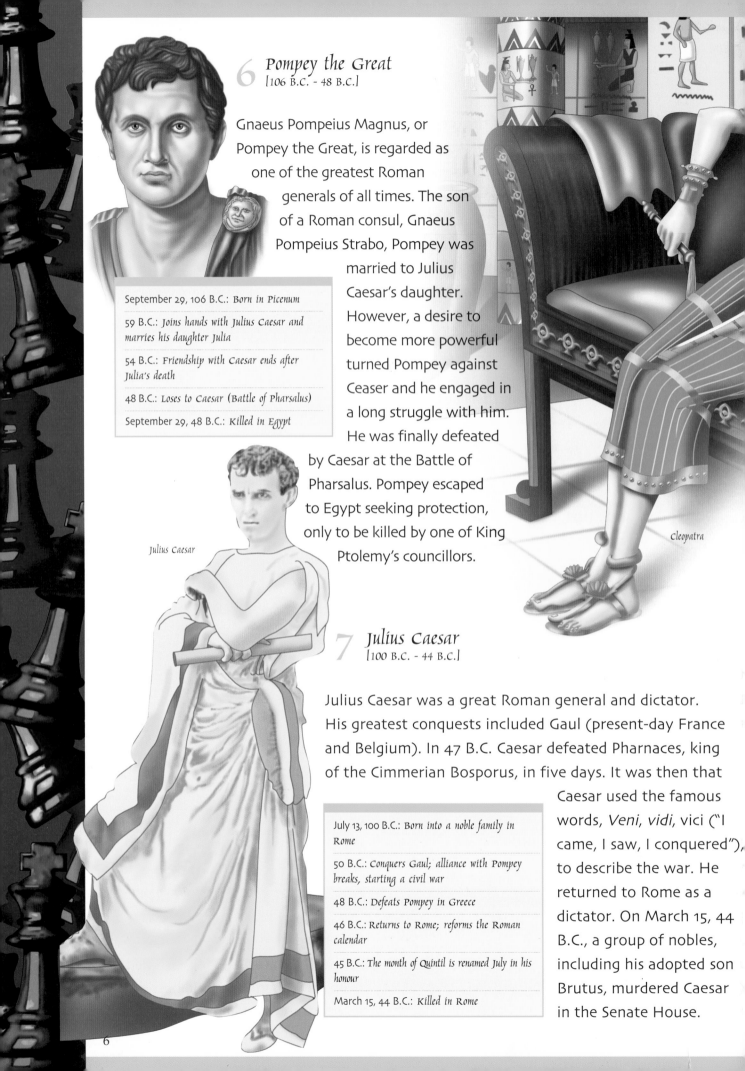

6 Pompey the Great
[106 B.C. - 48 B.C.]

Gnaeus Pompeius Magnus, or Pompey the Great, is regarded as one of the greatest Roman generals of all times. The son of a Roman consul, Gnaeus Pompeius Strabo, Pompey was married to Julius Caesar's daughter. However, a desire to become more powerful turned Pompey against Ceasar and he engaged in a long struggle with him. He was finally defeated by Caesar at the Battle of Pharsalus. Pompey escaped to Egypt seeking protection, only to be killed by one of King Ptolemy's councillors.

September 29, 106 B.C.: *Born in Picenum*

59 B.C.: *Joins hands with Julius Caesar and marries his daughter Julia*

54 B.C.: *Friendship with Caesar ends after Julia's death*

48 B.C.: *Loses to Caesar (Battle of Pharsalus)*

September 29, 48 B.C.: *Killed in Egypt*

Cleopatra

Julius Caesar

7 Julius Caesar
[100 B.C. - 44 B.C.]

Julius Caesar was a great Roman general and dictator. His greatest conquests included Gaul (present-day France and Belgium). In 47 B.C. Caesar defeated Pharnaces, king of the Cimmerian Bosporus, in five days. It was then that Caesar used the famous words, *Veni, vidi,* vici ("I came, I saw, I conquered"), to describe the war. He returned to Rome as a dictator. On March 15, 44 B.C., a group of nobles, including his adopted son Brutus, murdered Caesar in the Senate House.

July 13, 100 B.C.: *Born into a noble family in Rome*

50 B.C.: *Conquers Gaul; alliance with Pompey breaks, starting a civil war*

48 B.C.: *Defeats Pompey in Greece*

46 B.C.: *Returns to Rome; reforms the Roman calendar*

45 B.C.: *The month of Quintil is renamed July in his honour*

March 15, 44 B.C.: *Killed in Rome*

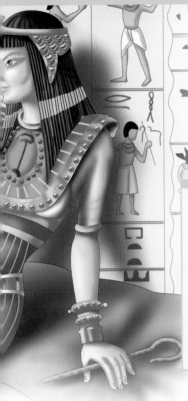

8 Cleopatra - Queen of Egypt
[69 B.C. - 31 B.C.]

Cleopatra succeeded her father Ptolemy XII Auletes to the throne and was the last pharaoh of Egypt. Known for her beauty, ambition and intelligence, she could speak nine languages! When Julius Caesar captured Egypt, she sought his help to regain control from her brother Ptolemy XIII. Following Caesar's death, she married his general, Marcus Anthony. When Augustus Caesar defeated Anthony at the Battle of Actium and conquered Alexandria, Cleopatra killed herself using a snake.

69 B.C.: *Born*

51 B.C.: *Succeeds to the throne along with her brother, Ptolemy XIII*

47 B.C.: *Becomes co-ruler with Ptolemy XIV, after having Ptolemy XIII killed with the help of Julius Caesar*

36 B.C.: *Marries Marcus Anthony*

31 B.C.: *Commits suicide after losing the Battle of Actium to Augustus*

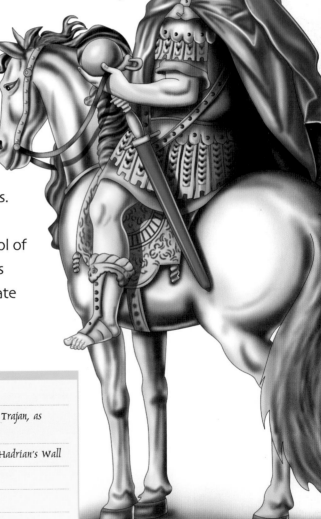

Augustus

9 Augustus Caesar
[63 B.C. - A.D. 14]

September 23, 63 B.C.: *Born as Gaius Octavius*

42 B.C.: *Defeats Caesar's assassins, Brutus and Cassius, in the final battle at Philippi*

September 2, 31 B.C.: *Defeats Marcus Anthony in a naval battle near Actium*

January 16, 27 B.C.: *Roman Senate gives him the title of Augustus*

12 B.C.: *Becomes pontifex maximus (head of the Roman religion) after the death of Lepidus*

August 19, A.D. 14: *Dies in Nola, near Naples; succeeded by stepson Tiberius*

Julius Caesar's great-nephew, Octavius, joined with Marcus Anthony and Marcus Aemilius Lepidus to kill his great-uncle's murderers. Later, though, Octavius fought Anthony for control of the empire and defeated him at the Battle of Actium. Octavius became the first emperor of Rome. In 27 B.C., the Roman Senate named him Augustus, meaning "the holy one".

10 Hadrianus
[76 - 138]

January 24, 76: *Born in Spain*

117: *Succeeds his adoptive father, Trajan, as emperor*

122: *Orders the construction of Hadrian's Wall*

132: *Suppresses uprising of Jews*

138: *Adopts Antoninus Pius*

July 10, 138: *Dies*

Publius Aelius Hadrianus, or Hadrian, was one of the "Five Good Emperors" of Rome. He brought stability and peace to his land. After suppressing a Jewish uprising, Hadrian declared Jerusalem a Roman city. He built the famous Hadrian's Wall, stretching 118 km (73 miles) across the north of Roman Britain and the Arch of Hadrian in Athens. He also rebuilt the Pantheon in Rome. On his death, Hadrian was succeeded by Antoninus Pius.

11 Marcus Aurelius
[121 - 180]

Marcus Aurelius belonged to the Nervan-Antonian dynasty of the Roman Empire. He was named Marcus Aurelius Antoninus when he was appointed heir to Emperor Antoninus Pius. A thoughtful and learned figure, Marcus is better known as a philosopher-king. The most famous of his works are the *Meditations*, written in Greek. He died in his military camp at Vindobona (Vienna) or Sirmium, Pannonia.

April 26, 121: *Born in Rome*

February 25, 138: *Adopted by his uncle, Emperor Antoninus Pius*

161: *Becomes Roman emperor; insists that adoptive brother Lucius Verus be made co-emperor*

169: *Verus dies of stroke*

177: *Marcus makes his 16-year-old son, Commodus, co-emperor*

March 17, 180: *Dies*

Marcus Aurelius

12 Zenobia
[Died after 274]

Zenobia reigned as queen of Palmyra in 267-272. She is believed to have murdered her husband Septimius Odenathus and obtained control of his lands for her son Vaballathus. She waged many wars, expanding her territory to East Asia Minor, Syria, northern Mesopotamia and Egypt. In 272, Roman Emperor Aurelian conquered Palmyra. Zenobia was captured and paraded on the streets of Rome. Later she was granted a villa in Tibur, where she spent the rest of her life.

267-272: *Rules Palmyra*

269: *Captures Egypt and proclaims herself queen of Egypt*

272: *Roman Emperor Aurelian defeats Zenobia and conquers her kingdom*

274: *Zenobia is captured and paraded in Rome*

13 Constantine the Great
[c. 280 - 337]

Constantine I was born to Roman Emperor Constantius I and Helena, an innkeeper's daughter. He reunited the Roman Empire after coming to power in 306. He was the first Roman emperor to support Christianity. He rebuilt the ancient Greek city of Byzantine, renamed it Nova Roma and made it his capital. It was renamed Constantinople after his death.

c. 280: *Born in Naissus, Moesia*

July 25, 306: *His troops name him Augustus*

315: *Conquers Greece and the Balkans*

May 11, 330: *Makes Byzantine (now Istanbul, Turkey) the capital of the Roman Empire*

May 22, 337: *Dies in Ancyrona, Bithynia; before his death, divides the empire among his three sons*

Constantine I

14 Attila the Hun
[406 - 453]

Attila

Attila and his brother Bleda succeeded their uncle as leaders of the Huns, a wandering tribe. It is believed that Attila killed his brother on a hunting trip to become the sole ruler. He then began terrorising Europe and Asia. His invasion of Gaul ended in defeat at the hands of the Romans and the Visigoths. Attila then invaded Italy. It is said that he did not capture Rome because of a request made by Pope Leo I.

406: Doubt still exists as to his exact year of birth

432: The Huns unite, for the first time, under Rua

434: Rua's nephews Attila and Bleda succeed him

445: Attila kills Bleda

447: Invades the Balkan provinces

September 20, 451: Defeated in the Battle of Chalons by the combined forces of Roman general Aetius and the Visigoths

452: Invades Italy, but does not capture Rome

453: Dies

Empress Theodora

15 Theodora
[c. 497 - 548]

c. 497: Born

525: Marries Justinian I

527: Becomes empress

532: Advises her husband on how to handle the Nika riots

548: Dies in Constantinople (now Istanbul, Turkey)

One of the greatest Byzantine rulers, Theodora was born to a bear keeper at the circus. She was an actress before she married Justinian I. When he succeeded to the throne, Theodora was proclaimed empress. An able leader, Theodora was responsible for crushing the Nika riots of 532. She also persuaded the emperor to change the laws to permit noblemen to marry lower-class women like her.

16 Maurice
[c. 539 - 602]

c. 539: Born in Cappadocia

582: Becomes emperor

591: Ends war with Persia

602: Killed by his soldiers on orders of Phocas

Maurice was a successful general who became the Byzantine emperor after the death of his father-in-law, Tiberius II. Maurice's rule was troubled by wars on all frontiers. Although he could not defeat the Lombards in Italy, he ended the war with Persia and restored Khusro II to the throne. Unfortunately, he failed to control the growing bitterness among his soldiers. He was overthrown and succeeded by a junior officer called Phocas.

Charlemagne

17 Charlemagne
[c.742 - 814]

April 2, c. 742: Born to the first Carolingian king, Pippin the Short

768: Becomes ruler with his brother Carloman

800: Crowned emperor by the Pope, in Rome

813: Makes son Louis I co-emperor

814: Dies; buried in the Aachen cathedral

Charlemagne ("Charles the Great") was the elder son of King Pippin III (the Short) of the Carolingian dynasty. On Pippin's death, Charlemagne and his brother Carloman became joint rulers. Carloman's death in 771 left Charlemagne the sole ruler of the Franks. In 800, on Christmas Day, Pope Leo III crowned him emperor. Literature, art and architecture flourished during his reign.

William I

18 William I
[c. 1027 - 1087]

Also called "William the Conqueror" and "William of Normandy", he was one of the greatest monarchs of England. At a very young age, he succeeded his father as the duke of Normandy. Later, William invaded England when Harold Godwinson, the earl of Wessex, succeeded King Edward to the throne. He defeated the earl at the Battle of Hastings to seize the throne.

c. 1027: Born in Falaise, Normandy, to Robert I, duke of Normandy and Arletta

1035: Becomes duke of Normandy

1047: Establishes power in Normandy by defeating rebel Norman barons with the help of King Henri I of France

October 14, 1066: At the famous Norman Conquest, William defeats King Harold

September 9, 1087: Dies after falling from a horse; buried at St. Stephen's Church, Caen

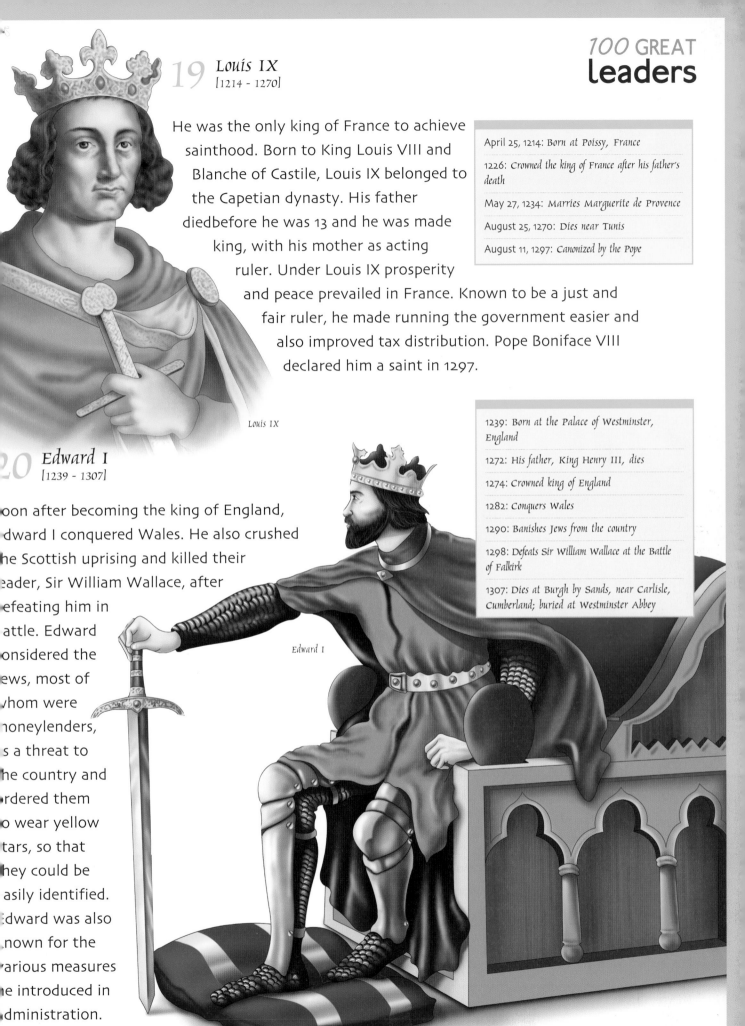

19 Louis IX
[1214 - 1270]

He was the only king of France to achieve sainthood. Born to King Louis VIII and Blanche of Castile, Louis IX belonged to the Capetian dynasty. His father died before he was 13 and he was made king, with his mother as acting ruler. Under Louis IX prosperity and peace prevailed in France. Known to be a just and fair ruler, he made running the government easier and also improved tax distribution. Pope Boniface VIII declared him a saint in 1297.

April 25, 1214: *Born at Poissy, France*

1226: *Crowned the king of France after his father's death*

May 27, 1234: *Marries Marguerite de Provence*

August 25, 1270: *Dies near Tunis*

August 11, 1297: *Canonized by the Pope*

Louis IX

20 Edward I
[1239 - 1307]

Soon after becoming the king of England, Edward I conquered Wales. He also crushed the Scottish uprising and killed their leader, Sir William Wallace, after defeating him in battle. Edward considered the Jews, most of whom were moneylenders, as a threat to the country and ordered them to wear yellow stars, so that they could be easily identified. Edward was also known for the various measures he introduced in administration.

1239: *Born at the Palace of Westminster, England*

1272: *His father, King Henry III, dies*

1274: *Crowned king of England*

1282: *Conquers Wales*

1290: *Banishes Jews from the country*

1298: *Defeats Sir William Wallace at the Battle of Falkirk*

1307: *Dies at Burgh by Sands, near Carlisle, Cumberland; buried at Westminster Abbey*

Edward I

Timur

21 Timur
[1336 - 1405]

Timur, also called Timurlenk ("Timur the Lame"), was a Mongol conqueror known for his savage conquests. The son of a tribal leader, Timur claimed he was related to Genghis Khan (creator of the Mongolian Empire). Timur conquered the territory between the Caspian and Black seas and invaded several Russian states. He also captured Persia and invaded India. However, his greatest victory came against the Ottoman Turks, capturing Sultan Bayazid I and destroying his army. Timur died on an expedition to invade China.

22 Ivan the Great
[1440 - 1505]

Ivan Vasilyevich, also called "Ivan the Great", was the grand prince of Moscow and the man responsible for uniting Russia. His greatest conquests included Tver and Novgorod. He freed Russia from the Tatars and put an end to threats of Mongol invasion. Ivan also formulated laws and promoted foreign artists. Monuments constructed in his time have a distinct Italian style.

Isabella I

23 Isabella I
[1451 - 1504]

Isabella I, the queen of Castile, married King Ferdinand II of Aragon in 1469. She and her husband established the "Spanish Inquisition" against the Jews and Moors (Muslims) who, despite converting to Christianity, continued to practise their original religion. She was also responsible for throwing Jews out of Spain, the conquest of Granada and the forced conversion of the Moors. A great patron of art, the queen extended her support to the famous explorer Christopher Columbus.

24 Maximilian I
[1459 - 1519]

Son of Emperor Frederick III, Maximilian I was the Holy Roman emperor and the king of Germany. As emperor, he introduced much-needed changes to the government and the army. He also joined the Holy League to counter the French and tried to expand his territory through the Italian Wars. Popular among his subjects, Maximilian promoted both science and the arts.

Maximilian I

Mary I

March 22, 1459: *Born in Vienna, Austria*

1477: *Marries Mary, heiress of Burgundy*

1493: *Succeeds his father, Frederick III, as the Holy Roman emperor*

January 12, 1519: *Dies in Wels, Upper Austria; succeeded by his grandson Charles V*

25 Mary I - Queen of England
[1516 - 1553]

Queen Mary I of England was the only child of King Henry VIII and Queen Catherine. Unlike her father, Mary was a strong Catholic. Immediately after becoming the queen, she tried to establish Roman Catholicism in England. Several popular Protestant leaders were executed in the process, earning her the title "Bloody Mary". At the end, her attempts proved to be largely unsuccessful.

February 18, 1516: *Born in Greenwich, London*

July 19, 1553: *Becomes queen after half-brother Edward VI dies*

1554: *Marries Philip II of Spain*

November 17, 1558: *Dies in London; succeeded by half-sister Elizabeth I*

26 Philip II
[1527 - 1598]

King of Spain and of Portugal, Philip II was born to Holy Roman Emperor Charles V and Isabella of Portugal. He became king after his father stepped down in 1556. In 1580, he invaded Portugal and seized power. During his reign, Spanish colonies were established in the Americas and the 60-year war with France ended, but his rule was also marked by financial instability and conflicts with England and the Netherlands.

May21, 1527: Born at Valladolid, Spain

1554: Marries Queen Mary I of England, after the death of his first wife

1556: Becomes king of Spain

1559: Signs the Peace of Cateau-Cambresis, ending the war with France

1598: His son Philip III succeeds him after his death

27 Elizabeth I
[1533 - 1603]

Elizabeth I was the last of the Tudors and succeeded Queen Mary I, who died childless. Several attempts were made to kill the Protestant queen, but Elizabeth survived and went on to become one of the most respected English monarchs. The arts, especially literature , flourished under her (Shakespeare lived during her time). Also called the "Virgin Queen", Elizabeth never married.

September 7, 1533: Born to King Henry VIII and his second wife, Anne Boleyn

1558: Succeeds Mary I as the queen of England

February 25, 1570: Excommunicated by the Pope Pius V; Ridolfo leads a Roman Catholic plot to kill the queen and replace her with Queen Mary I of Scotland

1587: Mary I of Scotland is executed

1588: Scores a decisive victory over the Spanish Armada, sent by King Philip II of Spain

March 24, 1603: Dies at Richmond Palace, Surrey, without naming her successor

28 Henry IV
[1553 - 1610]

The first Bourbon king of France, King Henry IV was the son of Antoine de Bourbon and Jeanne d'Albret, the queen of Navarra. A man of vision and courage, Henry promoted agriculture and industry, built several roads, bridges and canals and expanded foreign trade. He also promoted colonization of Canada. One of the most popular rulers of all times, Henry IV was killed by a fanatical Roman Catholic.

Henry IV

December 13, 1553: Born in Pau, Navarre

1584: Becomes legal heir to the French throne upon the death of the duke of Alencon

1589: After the death of King Henry III, the Catholic League prevents him from becoming king

July 25, 1593: Converts to Roman Catholicism

February 27, 1594: Crowned king of France

1578: Orders construction of Pont Neuf, the bridge across Seine River

May 14, 1610: Killed by Francois Ravaillac; buried at St. Denis Basilica

Oliver Cromwell

29 Oliver Cromwell
[1599 - 1658]

Oliver Cromwell was a soldier and statesman who also served as lord protector of England for several years. He defeated King Charles I in the First Civil War and supported his removal from Parliament. Cromwell was involved in the king's trial and, finally, his execution after the Second Civil War. Cromwell is also infamously associated with the mass murder of over 3,000 Irishmen in Drogheda after its capture. This only stirred up the English-Irish clash, which was to last for over three centuries.

April 25, 1599: Born in Huntingdon, England, to Robert Cromwell and Elizabeth Stewart

1628: Elected to Parliament

1647: Supports removal of Charles I from Parliament

1649: Massacres over 3,000 people, including Irish Royalist soldiers and Catholic priests, in Drogheda

1651: Approves the Navigation Act, which led to the first of the Dutch Wars

1657: Declines the kingship offered by Parliament

September 3, 1658: Dies in London; within two years Charles II is restored as king

Sir Walter Raleigh lays down his cloak for Queen Elizabeth I

30 Louis XIV
[1638 - 1715]

September 5, 1638: Born to King Louis XIII and Anne of Austria

May 14, 1643: Becomes king at the age of four

1661: Assumes power after the death of Cardinal Mazarin, the acting ruler

1672: Invades Holland, resulting in the Third Dutch War

May 6, 1682: Moves his court to Versailles

1688: Attacks the Holy Roman Empire

1689: Passes "Code Noir", allowing use of slaves in French colonies

September 1, 1715: Succeeded by his great-grandson Louis XV after his death

King Louis XIV ruled France from 1643 until his death in 1715. During his rule, France fought four major wars that expanded its boundaries and made it one of the most powerful states in Europe. Louis also promoted slavery in the French colonies and encouraged anti-Protestant activities. It is believed that his policies were largely responsible for the conditions leading to the French Revolution.

31 Peter I
[1672 - 1725]

Peter I

Peter the Great was the first emperor of Russia. He played a major role in the formation of modern Russia. As part of this exercise, he banned the traditional Russian dress, imposed taxes on beards and encouraged Russians to go abroad for education. During his rule, Russia was constantly at war – first with the Ottoman Empire and then with Charles XII of Sweden. He finally defeated Charles XII at Poltava, in 1709.

June 9, 1672: *Born to Czar Alexis and his second wife, Natalya Naryshkina*

1682: *Made tsar with his brother Ivan V*

1696: *Becomes sole ruler after death of Ivan V*

1700: *Loses the Battle of Narva against Charles XII of Sweden*

1703: *Founds the city of St. Petersburg*

1708: *Defeated by Charles XII at Golovchin*

June 27, 1709: *Defeats Charles XII at Poltava, forcing him to flee*

1721: *Russian Senate proclaims him the emperor*

February 8, 1725: *Dies in St. Petersburg*

32 Robert Walpole, 1st Earl of Orford
[1676 - 1745]

Regarded as the first British prime minister, Sir Robert Walpole served during the reigns of George I and George II. An able and shrewd statesman, Walpole adopted a policy of friendship even towards England's biggest rival, France. He introduced several economic reforms and promoted trade by encouraging the production of raw materials in the British colonies.

August 26, 1676: *Born in Norfolk, England*

1701: *Becomes member of Parliament*

1712: *Convicted of corruption and imprisoned*

1720: *Returns to office*

1721: *Appointed lord of the treasury*

1733: *Proposal of excise tax on wine and tobacco is defeated in parliament*

1742: *Forced to resign on charges of rigging the Chippenham by-election; created earl of Orford*

March 18, 1745: *Dies in London; earlier, presents his residence for use by future prime ministers*

33 Benjamin Franklin
[1706 - 1790]

A statesman of great standing, Franklin spent his early days writing and publishing. Later, pursuing his interest in science, he demonstrated that lightning is electrical and also invented the lightning rod. However, Franklin is most remembered for his role in the American Revolution. He negotiated the Treaty of Paris in 1783 and worked to put an end to slavery

January 17, 1706: *Born to a soap-maker in Boston*

1723: *Runs away from home and goes to Philadelphia*

1732: *Starts writing* Poor Richard's Almanack, *famous for sayings like "A penny saved is a penny earned"*

1751: *Establishes the Pennsylvania Hospital, the first hospital in independent United States*

1775: *Becomes the first U.S. postmaster general*

1787: *Participates in the Federal Constitutional Convention to formulate the U.S. Constitution*

April 17, 1790: *Dies; buried in the Christ Church burial grounds in Philadelphia*

34 William Pitt, the Elder (1st Earl of Chatham)
[1708 - 1778]

William Pitt was the secretary of state of England and also nominal prime minister twice, during the reigns of George II and George III. As head of the government from 1757, Pitt directed the defeat of France in India and Canada. However, he was forced to resign when King George III came to power in 1761. Pitt opposed the Treaty of Paris and criticised the government's policies towards the American colonies. At the same time, though, he was not in favour of granting them independence.

William Pitt

November 15, 1708: *Born in London*

1746: *Paymaster general of the forces in Henry Pelham's government*

1755: *Dismissed for criticising the government's war policies*

1756: *Recalled by George II; made secretary of State*

1757: *Becomes the prime minister of a coalition government*

1761: *Resigns from office*

1766: *Returns as prime minister; accepts title of earl of Chatham*

1768: *Resigns on account of ill health*

May 11, 1778: *Dies in Hayes, Kent; buried in Westminster Abbey*

Frederick II

The U.S. dollar with Benjamin Franklin potrait

35 Frederick II
[1712 - 1786]

January 24, 1712: *Born to King Frederick William I*

1740: *Succeeds his father as king of Prussia*

1740-48: *Involved in the War of the Austrian Succession*

August 17, 1786: *Friedrich Wilhelm II succeeds him upon his death*

Frederick the Great was the king of Prussia. Under him, Prussia flourished as a great European power. His dream of an independent Germany, however, did not come true until a century later. Often referred to as the "enlightened monarch", Frederick II brought about important changes to the law, promoted trade and encouraged education. He loved art and music. Being a flutist himself, he wrote many pieces of flute music.

36 Catherine II
[1729 - 1796]

Married to Tsar Peter III, Catherine II was more popular than her husband. She conspired to declare herself the ruler and, shortly afterwards, had the tsar killed. As empress of Russia, Catherine increased the power of the centre over rural areas and freed the nobles from taxes and state service. She was a keen supporter of the arts and literature and even wrote several comedies and stories.

George Washington

May 2, 1729: Born in Stettin, Prussia, to Prince Christian Augustus of Germany

1744: Marries the future tsar, Peter III

1762: Peter is killed six months after he becomes tsar; Catherine succeeds him

1778: Mediates between Prussia and Austria in the War of the Bavarian Succession

1780: Creates a group to defend neutral ships from attacks by Great Britain during the American Revolution

1783: Conquers Crimea after first war with the Ottoman Empire

1785: Issues charter freeing nobles from state service and taxes

November 17, 1796: Dies near St. Petersburg, Russia; succeeded by Paul I

37 George Washington
[1732 - 1799]

Called the "father of his country", George Washington was the first president of the United States. He played a major role in America's attainment of freedom. As president, he made several administrative reforms and was also involved in the creation of the US capital, District of Columbia (Washington, D.C.). He also crushed the Whisky Rebellion (1794) caused by the imposing of excise tax on whisky.

February 22, 1732: Born to Augustine Washington and Mary Ball, in Westmoreland, Virginia

1775: Assumes command of the Continental Army during the American Revolutionary War

1781: Defeats British troops under General Cornwallis at the Battle of Yorkham, putting an end to British hold over America

February 4, 1789: Elected president

1792: Elected president for the second term

February 25, 1793: Holds the first cabinet meeting

December 14, 1799: Dies; buried on his estate at Mount Vernon, Virginia

John Adams

38 John Adams
[1735 - 1826]

The second president of the United States, John Adams also played a key role in the drafting of the Massachusetts Constitution. In 1789-97, he had served as vice-president under George Washington. Adams became the president in 1797, after Washington refused to run for elections a third time. The term was marked by the unpopular Alien and Sedition Act, by which foreigners were forced out of the country and the freedom of the press was limited. This largely resulted in Adams's defeat in the next elections.

October 30, 1735: Born in Braintree, Massachusetts

1780: Frames the Massachusetts Constitution

April 21, 1789: Becomes the first vice-president of independent America

1797: Becomes president after defeating Thomas Jefferson

1798: Alien and Sedition Act passed

July 4, 1826: Dies in Quincy, Massachusetts, on the 50th anniversary of American independence

39 Thomas Jefferson
[1743 - 1826]

Horatio Nelson

The third president of the United States, Thomas Jefferson wrote the Declaration of Independence, announcing America's separation from Britain. He was the first president to work from the White House. The founder of the Democratic Party, he also developed the theory of states' rights, with lesser authority given to the federal government. In 1803, he helped in the purchase of Louisiana from France ("Louisiana Purchase").

April 13, 1743: Born in Shadwell, Virginia

1779: Becomes the governor of Virginia

1790: Becomes the secretary of state

1800: Takes office as president

1803: Launches the Lewis and Clarke Expedition to the U.S. Pacific coast

1809: Retires from public life

July 4, 1826: Dies in Monticello, Virginia

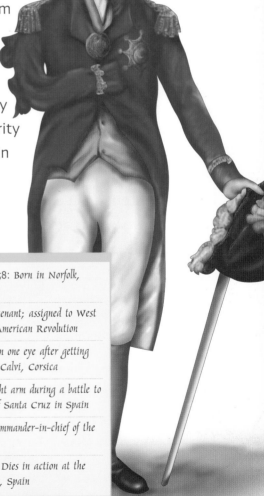

40 Horatio Nelson, Viscount
[1758 - 1805]

British commander Horatio Nelson is known for his victories over the French general Napoleon. One such was in the Battle of the Nile in 1798. By trapping Napoleon's fleets in Egypt, he ended Napoleon's attempts to attack the British in India. The greatest victory, however, was undoubtedly the Battle of Trafalgar. Nelson died in this battle, but not before defeating the joined forces of France and Spain.

September 29, 1758: Born in Norfolk, England

1777: Becomes lieutenant; assigned to West Indies during the American Revolution

1794: Loses sight in one eye after getting shot in a battle at Calvi, Corsica

1797: Loses his right arm during a battle to capture the town of Santa Cruz in Spain

1801: Appointed commander-in-chief of the British navy

October 21, 1805: Dies in action at the Battle of Trafalgar, Spain

41 Andrew Jackson
[1767 - 1845]

Andrew Jackson

The seventh president of the United States, he is known for his notorious decisions, especially the Indian Removal Act of 1830. Under this act, Native American tribes living east of the Mississippi River were driven out of their lands. Ignoring the Supreme Court ruling, Jackson sent military support to expel the native population. This eventually led to the infamous "Trail of Tears", in which about 4,000 Cherokees were killed enroute to Oklahoma.

March 15, 1767: Born to Andrew Jackson, sr. and Elizabeth Hutchinson, in Waxhaws region, South Carolina

1815: Defeats British troops at the Battle of New Orleans

1829: Elected president

1830: Passes the Indian Removal Act

1832: Dismantles the Bank of the United States

1835: Sends military support to remove the natives from their lands

January 30, 1835: The first-ever attempt to kill an American president

June 8, 1845: Dies in Tennessee

42 Napoleon Bonaparte
[1769 - 1821]

August 15, 1769: Born in Ajaccio, Corsica.

1798: His fleets are defeated at the Battle of the Nile

1804: Crowns himself emperor of France

May 26, 1805: Crowned king of Italy

1812: Invades Russia, but forced to retreat

1813: Suffers defeat at the Battle of the Nations against the Allied forces of Britain, Russia, Sweden, Spain, Portugal, Prussia, Austria and a few German states

March 31, 1814: Paris is occupied; in April Napoleon is forced to step down from the throne and is exiled to the island of Elba

February 26, 1815: Escapes from Elba and returns to Paris

June 18, 1815: Defeated at the Battle of Waterloo

May 5, 1821: Dies in exile on the island of St. Helena

Military dictator and the emperor of France, Napoleon was nicknamed "Little Corporal". His military ambitions cost the lives of millions. This made him unpopular, despite the fact that he introduced several lasting changes for the betterment of education, economy and laws. He conquered most of Western and Central Europe. However, his attempts to conquer Great Britain were foiled by Admiral Nelson. Napoleon was finally defeated by the duke of Wellington at the Battle of Waterloo.

Napoleon Bonaparte

43 *Alexander I of Russia*
[1777 - 1825]

To start with, Alexander I was a very broad-minded leader. He suppressed the secret police, lifted the ban on foreign travel and books, reformed education and improved the lives of slaves. Later, disillusioned by a farmers' revolt and betrayed by Napoleon, Alexander gave up his liberal views. Instead, he adopted a stricter approach and withdrew most of the reforms. He died mysteriously and was succeeded by his brother Nicholas I.

December 23, 1777: Born to Tsar Paul I and Maria Fedorovna

1801: Succeeds his father after the latter is killed

1807: Allies with Napoleon by the Treaty of Tilsit

1812: Napoleon invades Russia after a spate of political conflicts

1813: Participates in the Battle of the Nations against Napoleon

December 1, 1825: Dies at Taganrog

Alexander I

44 *Jose de San Martin*
[1778 - 1850]

This famous South American freedom fighter returned home from serving in the Spanish army, only to join the freedom struggle against Spain. San Martin first defeated the Spanish troops in Chacabuco in 1817. In 1818, he freed Chile by defeating the royalists at Maipu. He became the protector of Peru after capturing Lima in 1821, but soon retired from public life. He went to Europe in 1824, spending the rest of his life in poverty.

February 25, 1778: Born in Yapeyu, Argentina

1812: Joins revolution against Spain

1817: Defeats Spanish troops at Chacabuco

1818: Frees Chile

1821: Conquers Lima

1822: Meets Simon Bolivar, leaving him the task of completing the conquest of Peru

1850: Dies in self-imposed exile in France

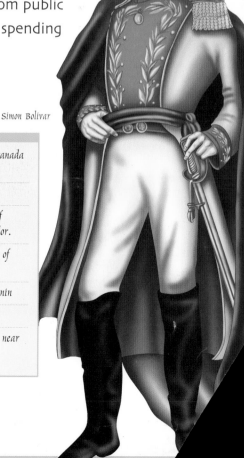

Simon Bolivar

45 *Simon Bolivar*
[1783 - 1830]

Simon Bolivar led independence struggles in Venezuela, Colombia, Panama, Ecuador, Peru and Bolivia. After serving under Napoleon for a while, Bolivar returned to Venezuela in 1807 and took active part in the revolution there. In 1819, he created Gran Colombia – consisting of countries free of Spanish control – and became its president. In 1822, he added Peru to the group. Bolivar resigned when the Gran Columbia collapsed in 1828.

July 24, 1783: Born in Caracas, New Granada (now Colombia, Venezuela and Ecuador)

1808: Joins the "resistance juntas"

1819: Creates Gran Colombia consisting of Venezuela, Colombia, Panama and Ecuador.

January 17, 1819: Proclaims the Republic of Colombia

1824: Decisively defeats the Spanish at Junin

1825: Bolivia is created in his honour

December 17, 1830: Dies of tuberculosis, near Santa Maria, Colombia

Abraham Lincoln
[1809 - 1865]

Abraham Lincoln was the 16th American president, whose anti-slavery views resulted in the four-year-long American Civil War. To suppress the revolt, Lincoln issued the Emancipation Proclamation under which slaves in the rebel states (southern states like Georgia) were freed. In his famous Gettysburg Address, he described democracy as "government of the people, by the people and for the people." On April 15, 1865, during a performance at Ford's Theatre, Lincoln was shot dead by actor John Wilkes-Booth.

Abraham
Lincoln

Otto von Bismarck
[1815 - 1898]

Otto von Bismarck was prime minister of the Kingdom of Prussia and the first chancellor of the German Empire. Through a series of wars, he fulfilled King Frederick's dream of a unified Germany. An old-fashioned politician, Bismarck fought the pro-working class (socialist) movements by banning several organisations. However, he also introduced several economic reforms, including pensions, health and accident insurance, limiting of women and child labour and setting down maximum working hours.

Otto von
Bismarck

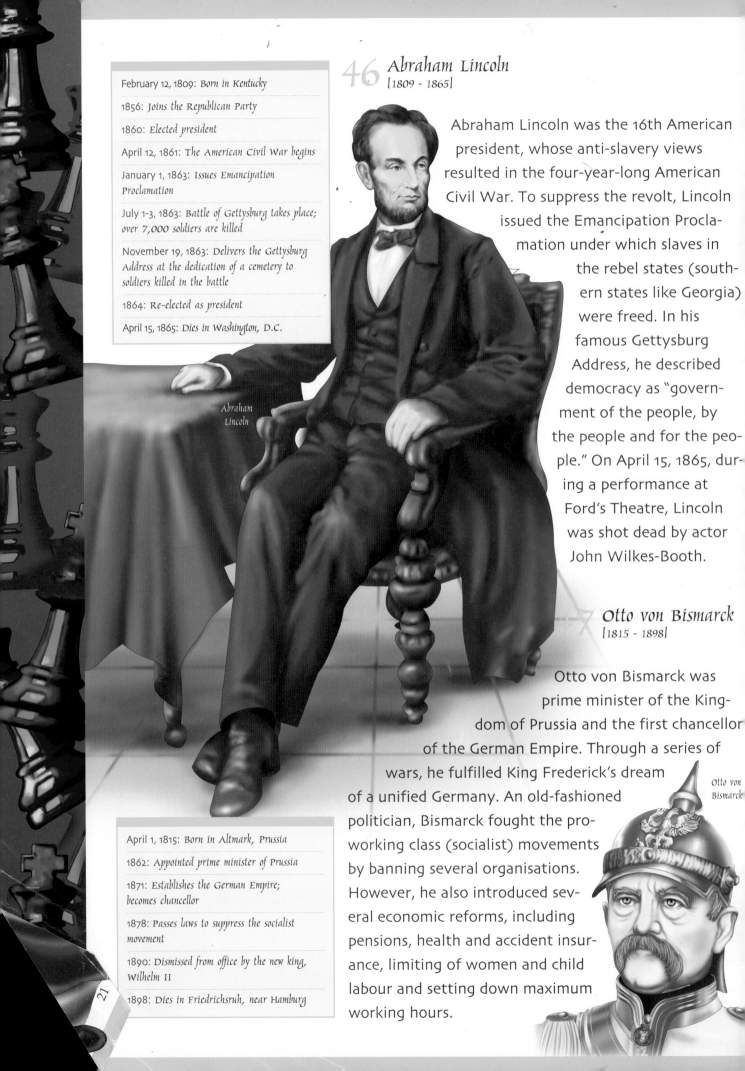

48 Victoria - Queen Of England
[1819 - 1901]

Queen Victoria ruled Great Britain for a record 63 years! Her rule saw a huge expansion of the British Empire. Devoted to her husband, Prince Albert, she withdrew from public life for three years after his death. This earned her the nickname "Widow of Windsor". At the persuasion of Prime Minister Benjamin Disraeli, she finally made a comeback and accepted the title of Empress of India. She was succeeded by her eldest son Edward VII.

May 24, 1819: Born to Edward Augustus, duke of Kent and Princess Victoria of Saxe-Coburg-Saalfield

June 20, 1837: Succeeds William IV at the age of 18

February 10, 1840: Marries her cousin, Prince Albert

1861: Withdraws from public life after Prince Albert's death

January 1, 1877: Becomes Empress of India

January 22, 1901: Dies at Osborne House on the Isle of Wight

Queen Victoria

49 Harriet Tubman
[1820 - 1913]

She played a major role in ending slavery in America. Born into slavery in Maryland, Tubman escaped in 1849 to become a defender of slaves. She led more than 300 hundred slaves to freedom through the 'Underground Railroad', forcing the weaker ones with a loaded revolver. During the civil war, Tubman served as a nurse and a spy for the Union forces in South Carolina.

1820: Born in Dorchester.

1849: Escapes slavery.

1861: Serves in the Union forces as a nurse during the civil war.

March 10, 1913: Dies in the home for needy blacks founded by her in Auburn, New York

50 Henri Marie La Fontaine
[1854 - 1943]

Henri Marie La Fontaine

La Fontaine was a Belgian senator for 36 years and was devoted to international peace. As a senator, he was responsible for various ground-breaking efforts to improve education, labor and foreign affairs. He supported the adoption of an eight hour day and forty hours working week. He also supported the League of Nations and disarmament. A part of the organized peace movement since the early 1880's, he won the Nobel Peace Prize in 1913.

April 11, 1854: Born in Brussels.

1895: Becomes a senator for the first time.

1897: Submits a bill on mine inspection.

1907: Becomes President of the International Peace bureau.

1913: Receives Nobel Peace Prize.

1926: Supports eight hour a day work programme.

1920: Attends the First Assembly of League of Nations.

May 14, 1943: Dies before Belgium is liberated.

Woodrow Wilson

51 Woodrow Wilson
[1856 - 1924]

As the 28th U.S. president, Wilson faced his biggest challenge during World War I. Although he kept America away from the war in the beginning, he was forced to join it in 1916. After the war, he began a strong movement for peace. In his famous "Fourteen Points" address, Wilson came up with the idea of the League of Nations. This was implemented during the Paris Peace Conference in 1919 and Wilson was awarded the Nobel Prize for Peace.

December 28, 1856: Born in Staunton, Virginia, U.S.

1912: Becomes president

1914: Decides not to participate in World War I

1916: Re-elected as president

April 6, 1917: Joins World War I by declaring war on Germany

January 8, 1918: Makes his Fourteen Points speech

1919: His idea of a League of Nations included in the Treaty of Versailles; awarded the Nobel Prize for Peace

October 2, 1919: A stroke leaves him partially paralysed

1921: Retires from the White House

February 3, 1924: Dies in Washington, D.C.

52 Theodore Roosevelt
[1858 - 1919]

Theodore Roosevelt became the U.S. president in 1901, when President William McKinley was killed. Considered to be the first "conservation" president, Roosevelt established the United States Forest Service, 51 bird reserves, 150 national forests and 5 national parks. Fondly called Teddy, he once refused to kill a bear cub during a hunting trip, after which toy manufacturers started naming teddy bears after him!

Theodore Roosevelt

October 27, 1858: Born in New York City

September 14, 1901: Becomes president

1904: Re-elected as president

1906: Wins Nobel Prize for Peace for the Russo-Japanese peace treaty

October 14, 1912: Escapes an attempt to kill him; doctors refuse to remove the bullet in his chest since it can prove fatal

January 6, 1919: Dies at Oyster Bay, Nassau county, New York

Karl Branting

53 Karl Hjalmar Branting
[1860 - 1925]

Regarded as the father of socialism (movement for workers' rights) in Sweden, Branting was also the nation's prime minister. He upheld the rights of workers and criticised laws against unions. Although he insisted on Sweden staying out of World War I, he participated in the Paris Peace Conference and got his country into the League of Nations. He was also involved in drafting the Geneva Protocol to settle international disputes legally. In 1921, he shared the Nobel Prize for Peace with Christian Louis Lange.

November 23, 1860: Born in Stockholm

1889: Forms the Social Democratic Labour Party

1920: Becomes prime minister

October 1920: Dissolves parliament; loses the elections

1921: Returns as prime minister; wins Nobel Prize for Peace

1924: Becomes prime minister for the third time

January 1925: Resigns from office due to illness

February 24, 1925: Dies in Stockholm

54 Douglas Hyde
[1860 - 1949]

Douglas Hyde was an Irish scholar and politician. He helped revive Irish language and literature by setting up the Gaelic League in 1893. The league went on to produce great leaders like Eamon de Valera and Michael Collins. In 1938, Hyde became the first president of Ireland and held office until 1945. He wrote several books, the most famous being *A Literary History of Ireland* and *The Love Songs of Connacht*.

January 17, 1860: Born in Frenchpark, in County Roscommon, Ireland

1909-32: Teaches modern Irish

1938: Becomes the first president of Ireland

April 1940: Suffers stroke and is confined to the wheelchair

June 24, 1945: Retires due to ill health

July 12, 1949: Dies in Dublin, Ireland

Douglas Hyde

55 Aristide Briand
[1862 - 1932]

March 28, 1862: Born in Nantes, France

1905: Passes the law of separation of church and state

1906: Becomes minister of education and religion

1909: Becomes premier for the first of 11 times

1925: Co-authors the Locarno Pact

1926: Shares the Nobel Prize for Peace with Stresemann

1928: Drafts the Kellog-Briand pact banning war

March 7, 1932: Dies in Paris, France

Briand became the French premier in 1909. He participated in the movement for labour-union formation and also in drafting the law of separation of church and state. A tireless supporter of international peace, Briand was criticised for trying to make peace with Germany. However, it was Briand who played a leading role in formulating the Locarno Pact – a treaty intended to establish peace in western Europe and ease relations with Germany.

October 16, 1863: Born in Birmingham,
Warwickshire, England

1915: Becomes Secretary of State for India.

1921: Becomes leader of the Conservative Party

1924: Becomes secretary of state for foreign affairs

1925: Awarded the Nobel Peace Prize for his
role in the Locarno Pact

March 17, 1937: Dies of apoplexy in London

56 Sir Austen Chamberlain
[1863 - 1937]

Sir Chamberlain was a British politician, most
remembered for his contributions to world peace.
Although he opposed the League of Nations' Geneva
Protocol (1924), Chamberlain was actively involved
in the formulation of the
Locarno Pact. He also had
the foresight to predict that
Hitler would be the greatest
threat to world peace.
Although he did not hold a
cabinet position after 1931,
he continued to be an
influential figure.

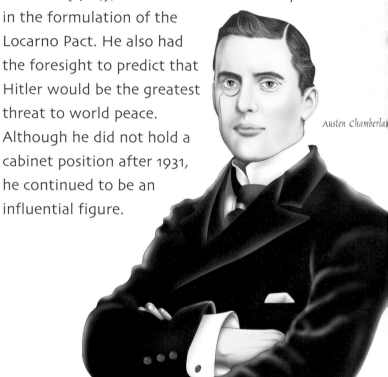

Mahatma Gandhi

Austen Chamberla

57 Mohandas Karamchand Gandhi
[1869 - 1948]

Also known as "Mahatma" ("Great Soul"), Gandhi
was the key figure in India's freedom struggle. His prin-
ciples of satyagraha and non-violence have influenced
leaders like Martin Luther King and Nelson Mandela. Gandhi
led such simple and non-
violent – yet effective –
movements as the Dandi
March and Quit India. He
was an ardent supporter
of Hindu-Muslim unity.
Ironically, he was killed by
a fanatic who was angered
by his concern for the
Muslims.

October 2, 1869: Born in Porbandar, Gujarat,
India

April 5, 1930: Leads thousands to the sea to
collect salt, in the famous Dandi March

1942: Starts the Quit India movement;
imprisoned for two years.

August 15, 1947: India becomes independent;
Pakistan splits from India to form a separate
Muslim country

January 30, 1948: Killed by Nathuram
Godse in New Delhi, India

58 Vladimir Ilyich Lenin
[1870 - 1924]

A Russian revolutionary, Lenin was the founder of Bolshevism (later the Russian Communist Party). After returning from exile, Lenin organised the Socialist Revolution of October 1917 and subsequently established a Soviet government. The new government took control of banks and industry. It also put an end to private ownership of land and gave farmers and workers more rights. After his death, Lenin was succeeded by Stalin.

Vladimir Ilyich Lenin

1870: Born Vladimir Ilyich Ulyanov at Simbirsk, Russia

1895: Exiled to Siberia

1900: Leaves Russia

October 1917: Lenin returns to Russia to overthrow Aleksandr Kerensky's government

1921: Launches the New Economic Policy allowing private companies to operate

January 21, 1924: Dies of a stroke, in Gorki, near Moscow, Russia

59 Arthur Griffith
[1871 - 1922]

March 31, 1871: Born in Dublin

1899: Founds a newspaper, the United Irishman

1905: Founds Sinn Fein

August 12, 1922: Dies in Dublin, at the beginning of the civil war

Griffith was the founder of Sinn Fein, the famous political wing of the Irish Republican Army. He fought for the creation of two different governments for England and Ireland, to be headed by one common monarch – namely, the king of England. Elected to the parliament in 1918, he was also responsible for the Anglo-Irish Treaty (1921) establishing the Irish Free State.

60 Cordell Hull
[1871 - 1922]

The U.S. secretary of state for 12 years, Cordell Hull worked for the improvement of international relations. He helped in signing peace and trade agreements with several countries. He also promoted the Good Neighbor Policy towards Latin America, giving it financial help. During World War II, he backed the establishment of a world organisation to maintain peace. In 1913 Hull introduced the first Federal Income Tax bill.

October 2, 1871: Born in Overton county, Tennessee

1930: Elected to the U.S. Senate

1933: Appointed secretary of state

1944: Resigns from his post

1945: Wins the Nobel Prize for Peace; serves as senior adviser to the American delegation to the United Nations conference in San Francisco

July 23, 1955: Dies in Bethesda, Maryland, U.S.

Cordell Hull

Winston Churchill

61 Winston Churchill
[1874 - 1965]

As the British prime minister during World War II, Churchill took an aggressive stand against Hitler. He also opposed the Indian independence struggle and viewed the Soviet Union as a threat. He put an end to the government's control over steel and auto industries introduced by the Labour Party. One of the greatest public figures of recent times, Churchill was also a great writer and received the Nobel Prize for Literature in 1953.

1874: Born in Oxfordshire, England
May 1940: Becomes the prime minister after Neville Chamberlain resigns
1945: Loses the elections to Labor Party
1951: Returns as the prime minister
1953: Receives knighthood
1955: Resigns, but remains member of parliament
1963: President Kennedy offers him honorary citizenship of the United States
1965: Dies in London

62 Gustav Stresemann
[1878 - 1929]

Founder of the German People's Party, Stresemann, was also chancellor and foreign minister in the Weimar Republic (German government). Although he supported the monarchy during World War I, Stresemann realised the need to improve relations between Germany and its enemy nations and actively campaigned to achieve this. He renewed the Rapallo Treaty with Russia and got Germany admitted into the League of Nations as a great power. He won the 1926 Nobel Prize for Peace for his contribution to the Locarno Pact.

May 10, 1878: Born in Berlin, Germany
1907: Enters the Reichstag
1918: Founds the German People's Party
1923: Becomes chancellor
1924: Becomes foreign minister
1926: Germany is admitted into the League of Nations
October 3, 1929: Dies in Berlin after suffering a stroke

63 Leon Trotsky
[1879 - 1940]

1879: Born to Jewish parents in Yanovka, Ukraine
October 1917: Organises the socialist revolution
1922: Stalin succeeds Lenin as leader of the party
1928: Expelled from the party by Stalin
1929: Banished from Russia; given asylum by Turkey
1935: Moves to Norway
December 1936: Soviet government gets him expelled from Norway; moves to Mexico
August 20, 1940: Killed in Coyoacan, Mexico

Trotsky was a Russian leader who played a prominent role in the 1917 Russian Revolution that brought the Bolsheviks into power. He was also the founder of the Red Army. Trotsky opposed Stalin's plan for "socialism in one country", meant to make the Soviet Union the only world power. This led to his exile from the country. In 1940 he was killed in Mexico by Ramon Mercader, a Spanish communist believed to be Stalin's agent.

Joseph Stalin

64 Joseph Stalin
[1879 - 1953]

After succeeding Lenin as leader of the Soviet Union, Stalin launched a campaign of terror to end all opposition. Old Bolshevik leaders, who opposed Stalin, were tried and executed in the 1930s. The failed Nazi invasion in 1941 further strengthened Stalin's position. After defeating Hitler, he continued his brutalities. Although Stalin is best remembered for his reign of terror and dictatorship, his economic reforms like the Five-Year Plan improved the financial condition of the country.

Douglas MacArthur

1879: *Born to a shoemaker in Gori, Georgia*

1922: *Succeeds Lenin as leader of the Bolsheviks*

1934: *Joins League of Nations*

1939: *Signs non-aggression pact with Germany*

1941: *Hitler invades Russia*

March 5, 1953: *Dies of cerebral haemorrhage, in Moscow*

65 Douglas MacArthur
[1880 - 1951]

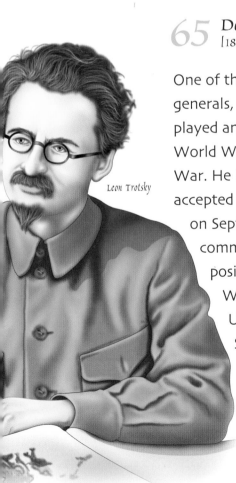

Leon Trotsky

One of the greatest American generals, Douglas MacArthur played an important role during World War II and the Korean War. He liberated the Philippines, accepted the surrender of Japan on September 2, 1945 and commanded the Allied forces positioned there. In the Korean War, as the commander of U.N. military forces in South Korea, he drove the North Korean forces out. However, his aggressive methods forced President Truman to recall him.

1880: *Born in Little Rock, Arkansas, U.S.*

1906-07: *Aide to President Theodore Roosevelt*

1935: *Heads the American military mission to the Philippines Commonwealth*

1941: *Returns to command U.S. forces in East Asia*

1944: *Promoted to the rank of general*

September 2, 1945: *Accepts Japan's surrender aboard USS Missouri*

1950: *Appointed commander of U.N. military forces in South Korea*

April 1951: *Removed from command*

April 5, 1964: *Dies in Washington, D.C.*

66 George Catlett Marshall
[1880 - 1959]

George Marshall

An American general and cabinet member, George Marshall made valuable contributions during times of both war and peace. During World War II, he directed the conquest of Germany. After the war he was appointed special ambassador to China. He promoted the "Marshall Plan" to improve post-war European economy. This plan also led to the formation of the North Atlantic Treaty Organisation (NATO).

December 31, 1880: *Born in Uniontown, Pennsylvania*

1919-24: *Serves in the army during World War I*

September 1939: *Becomes chief of army staff*

1944: *Promoted to the rank of general*

January 1947: *Made secretary of state*

July 1947: *Marshall Plan is proposed*

January 1949: *Resigns due to ill health*

September 1950: *Returns as secretary of defense*

September 1951: *Resigns from the post*

1953: *Wins the Nobel Prize for Peace*

October 16, 1959: *Dies in Washington, D.C.*

67 Kemal Atatürk
[1881 - 1938]

March 12, 1881: *Born in Salonika, Greece*

1919: *Forms the Turkish Nationalist Republican Party*

October 29, 1923: *Turkish Republic is founded; Atatürk is elected president*

1924: *Abolishes the caliphate*

November 10, 1938: *Dies in Istanbul, Turkey*

Atatürk ("father of Turks") was the founder and the first president of the Republic of Turkey. He formed the Turkish Nationalist Republican Party, which overthrew the Ottoman Empire and defeated the Greeks. After coming to power in 1923, Atatürk launched a variety of reforms. He replaced the Law of Islam with the Swiss Civil Code, thus separating religion and the state. He also simplified the Turkish script, helping to increase literacy.

68 Franklin D. Roosevelt
[1882 - 1945]

Franklin Roosevelt

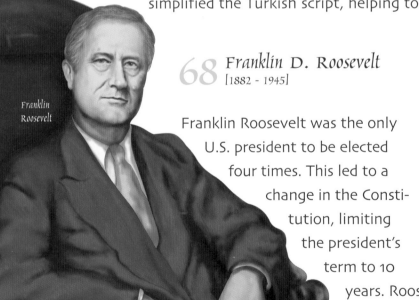

Franklin Roosevelt was the only U.S. president to be elected four times. This led to a change in the Constitution, limiting the president's term to 10 years. Roosevelt balanced the country's economy during the Great Depression (a period of great financial difficulty after World War I). providing support for elderly citizens and those who earned less money.

January 30, 1882: *Born in Hyde Park, New York*

1933: *Becomes the president*

1935: *Introduces the Social Security system, providing support for elderly citizens and for those who earn less*

January 6, 1941: *Makes his famous State of the Union Address, also called the 'Four Freedoms' Speech.*

December 7, 1941: *Japanese attack Pearl Harbor.*

April 12, 1945: *Dies in Warm Springs, Georgia*

69 Eamon de Valera
[1880 - 1959]

Eamon de Valera was the Prime Minister and President of Ireland. He is famous for his role in the Easter Rising of 1916. He was very passionate about his cause and refused to accept the Anglo-Irish Treaty and the Irish Free State since it excluded Northern Ireland and demanded loyalty to the British Monarchy. During his term, a new constitution declaring Ireland a fully independent state was introduced. He also kept Ireland neutral during World War II.

nito ussolini

October 14, 1882: Born in New York City

1913: Joins the newly founded group called Irish Volunteers

1916: Leads a Volunteer unit in the Easter Rising

1917: Elected Member of Parliament and becomes the President of Sinn Fein

June 1922: Start of the Irish Civil War

1926: Forms a new party called Fianna Fail or Soldiers of Destiny

1932: Becomes the Prime Minister following his party's win in elections

1959: Becomes President of Ireland

1973: Retires at the age of 91

1975: Dies in a Dublin nursing home soon after his wife's death

Eamon de Valera

70 Benito Mussolini
[1883 - 1945]

Mussolini was an Italian dictator and the founder of fascism (a kind of dictatorship). He believed this would strengthen the nation. He kept an iron control over the press and suppressed opposition using force. He replaced the parliamentary system with absolute dictatorship and encouraged terrorism. He glorified war and later joined hands with Hitler, calling the alliance Axis Powers. But following Italy's defeat in World War II and Germany's collapse in 1945, Mussolini was captured by anti-fascists and shot dead.

July 29, 1883: Born in Predappio, Romagna.

November 1914: Founds the newspaper called The Italian People.

1919: Fascism emerges as an organized political movement.

1922: Becomes the Premier of Italy.

1928: Ends the Parliamentary system of government.

1935: Allies with Germany.

1936: Aids Francisco Franco in the Spanish Civil War.

1939: Rome-Berlin Axis is formed.

1940: Italy enters World War II.

1943: Allies invasion turns Mussolini's colleagues against him and he loses power.

April 28, 1945: After the German collapse he is caught and shot.

71 Adolf Hitler
[1889 - 1945]

Hitler was a German dictator and the founder of Nazism. He was responsible for World War II and the Holocaust, a period when over 6 million Jews were killed. Hitler believed that the Germans belonged to the superior Aryan race and were meant to rule the world. Those who opposed him were tortured and killed in concentration camps. He killed himself in his Berlin mansion on April 30, 1945, to avoid capture by the Russians.

Adolf Hitler

Michael Collins

April 20, 1889: *Born in a small town near Linz, Upper Austria.*

1919: *Joins German's Workers' Party and renames it National socialist German Workers' Party or the Nazi Party.*

1934: *Proclaims himself Fuhrer (Leader).*

September 1, 1939: *Invades Poland starting World War II.*

June 1941: *Attacks USSR disregarding the non-aggression pact between the two nations.*

1943: *Defeated at the Battle of Stalingrad.*

April 29, 1945: *Marries Eva Braun.*

April 30, 1945: *Both commit suicide in Hitler's Berlin Bunker.*

72 Michael Collins
[1890 - 1922]

Considered a legend in Irish History, Michael Collins' contribution to the creation of the present Republic of Ireland is invaluable. Like most great Irish leaders, Collins became famous during the Easter Rising. After a prolonged struggle, Collins, along with Arthur Griffiths negotiated and signed the Anglo-Irish Treaty that set up the Irish Free State. He served as the Minister for Finance in the new government for a short while. He was killed by Republicans during the Civil War.

October 16, 1890: *Born in Sam's Cross, West Cork*

November 1909: *Joins the Irish Republican Brotherhood.*

1916: *Participates in the Easter Rising.*

1918: *Becomes the Member of Parliament.*

January 1919: *Organises the Irish Republican Army and leads it in the Irish War of Independence.*

December 1921: *Negotiates and signs the Anglo-Irish Treaty.*

June 1922: *Irish Civil War begins.*

August 22, 1922: *Killed in an ambush in County Cork. He was barely 32 years old.*

73 *Ho Chi Minh*
[1890 - 1969]

Ho Chi Minh was a famous Vietnamese freedom fighter who fought to free North Vietnam from France and other foreign forces. He led the Viet Minh independence movement of 1941, successfully driving the Japanese and the French out. He became the President of the Democratic Republic of Vietnam in 1954. However, he continued to fight to re-unite North and South Vietnam until his death in 1969.

Ho Chi Minh

May 19, 1890: *Born in Vietnam.*

1911: *Leaves Vietnam working on a French ship.*

1920: *Founds the French Communist Party.*

September 1945: *Proclaims the republic of Vietnam but agrees it will remain an autonomous state in the French Union.*

1954: *After defeating France becomes President of North Vietnam and soon after engages in battle to re-unite North and South Vietnam.*

74 *Dwight D. Eisenhower*
[1890 - 1969]

Nicknamed 'Ike', Dwight Eisenhower was an American President and the General of the United States Army. As the President, Eisenhower enforced 'desegregation' in schools to allow the admission of black students. He spent very little money on the military and ended the Korean War by signing agreements with Korea and China. Though the US was not involved in any major military activity during his term, there was an increase in the nuclear arms race.

October 14, 1890: *Born in Denison, Texas.*

December 1943: *Made Supreme Commander of the Allied forces in World War II.*

1952: *Elected as President.*

1953: *Helps achieve ceasefire in the Korean War.*

1956: *Passes the Interstate Highway Act.*

1957: *Enforces desegregation by sending troops to Little Rock Arkansas when its Governor refused entry of black students into Little Rock Central High School.*

March 28, 1969: *Dies in Washington D C.*

75 *Charles de Gaulle*
[1890 - 1970]

Charles de Gaulle

General Charles de Gaulle was the leader of the Free French forces during World War II and the first President of the Fifth Republic. He introduced tough measures to improve the economy of France after the war and ordered the making of a new constitution. Under him, France became politically stable and gained importance in the international stage. He also improved relations with China and Germany. He retired in 1969 following the defeat of his motion to change the constitution.

November 22, 1890: *Born in Lille, France.*

1940: *Founds the Free French Forces.*

1958: *Formation of the Fifth Republic.*

January 1959: *Becomes the President of the Fifth Republic.*

April 28, 1969: *Retires to Colombey-les-deux-Églises, where he dies a year later.*

76 Khan Abdul Ghaffar Khan
[1890 - 1988]

Known as 'Badshah Khan' (Khan of Khans), Ghaffar Khan was a Pathan leader famous for his non-violent opposition of British rule. His goal was a united and independent India. To achieve this, he founded the 'Khudai Khidmatgar' (meaning 'Servants of God') in 1929. He was inspired by Gandhi and viewed his own struggle as a Jihad (religious war) with only the enemy holding swords. He died in Peshawar in 1988.

1890: Born into a Pathan family in Charsadda, Afghanistan.

September 1929: Founds the 'Khudai Khidmatgar'.

1987: Awarded Bharat Ratna – India's highest civilian award.

January 18, 1988: Dies at Peshawar, and is buried in Jalalabad, Afghanistan.

77 Francisco Franco
[1892 - 1975]

This Spanish military dictator rose to power in the 1930's by winning the Spanish Civil War. He did so with the help of Hitler and Mussolini. However, Franco kept Spain out of World War II. After the war, Franco befriended the U.S. by allowing it to set up military bases in Spain during the Cold War. Franco remained in power until his death despite growing hatred towards him.

December 4, 1892: Born in El Ferrol, Spain.

1926: Becomes the youngest General ever in a European Army.

July 17, 1936: Leads a military uprising starting the Spanish Civil War.

March 28, 1939: Conquers Madrid ending the Civil War.

1947: Declares Spain a Monarchy but does not name a King until later in 1969.

1955: Spain enters the United Nations.

November 20, 1975: Dies in Madrid, Portugal

Francisco Franco

78 Mao Tse-Tung
[1893 - 1976]

Mao Tse-Tung was the founder of the People's Republic of China. He led the Communist Party to power after winning the Chinese Civil War. He also built the Red Army and was responsible for uniting China. He has, however, been criticized for his terrible economic and political decisions taken while in power, one of which was the 'Great Leap Forward' program that resulted in widespread starvation. Despite his faults, Mao continues to be worshipped in China.

December 26, 1893: Born in Shaoshan, Hunan Province, China.

1926: Chinese Civil War between the Communists and Kuomintang begins.

1927: Leads the Autumn Harvest Uprising at Changsha, Hunan and barely escapes death.

1931-34: Establishes the Chinese Soviet Republic.

1934-35: Leads the Red Army on the famous Long March emerging as a Communist leader.

1937-1945: Sino-Japanese War

1949: Establishes the People's Republic of China after defeating the Kuomintang in the Civil War

1958: Launches the 'Great Leap Forward' program

1966: Starts the Cultural Revolution to re-establish himself

September 9, 1976: Dies in Beijing, China

79 Nikita Sergeyevich Khrushchev
[1894 - 1971]

Leader of the Soviet Union, Nikita Khrushchev condemned Stalin saying he was responsible for mass murders. On becoming the Premier, Khrushchev crushed the Hungarian revolution. He also started the space program that launched Sputnik I and Yuri Gagarin into space. He is said to have demanded an apology from the U.S. President Eisenhower for flying U-2 spy planes over USSR. He was removed from office after the Cuban missile crisis, following his decision to place nuclear missiles in Cuba to threaten America.

Nikita Sergeyevich Khrushchev

April 17, 1894: *Born in Kalinovka, Kursk Province, Russia*

March 27, 1958: *Becomes the Premier of the Soviet Union*

May 16, 1960: *Demands apology from US ending the Big Four summit in Paris*

May 1962: *Decides to place nuclear missiles in Cuba following similar acts by US in Turkey, threatening the USSR*

October 15, 1962: *The thirteen days Cuban Missile Crisis begins. Soviet Union agrees to pull out after US agrees to do the same in Turkey*

1964: *Removed from office and placed under house arrest*

September 11, 1971: *Dies at his home in Moscow after seven years of house arrest*

80 Ayatollah Ruhollah Khomeini
[1900 - 1989]

Khomeini was an Iranian religious leader. He came to power by overthrowing Mohammed Reza Pahlavi, the then Shah of Iran. Khomeini's rule ended western influence in Iran. Shia Islamic Law was instituted with strict dress codes, press was suppressed and women lost their rights as equal citizens. Iraqi leader Saddam Hussein felt threatened by the spread of Khomeini's ideology and invaded Iran, thus beginning the decade-long Iran-Iraq War.

Ayatollah Ruhollah Khomeini

May 17, 1900: *Born as Ruhollah Mousavi in Khomeyn, Iraq*

1964: *Exiled from Iran for criticizing the Shah*

February 1, 1979: *Returns to Iran to join the Iranian Revolution*

February 11, 1979: *Seizes power*

September 22, 1980: *Start of the Iran-Iraq War.*

June 3, 1989: *Dies in Tehran, Iran*

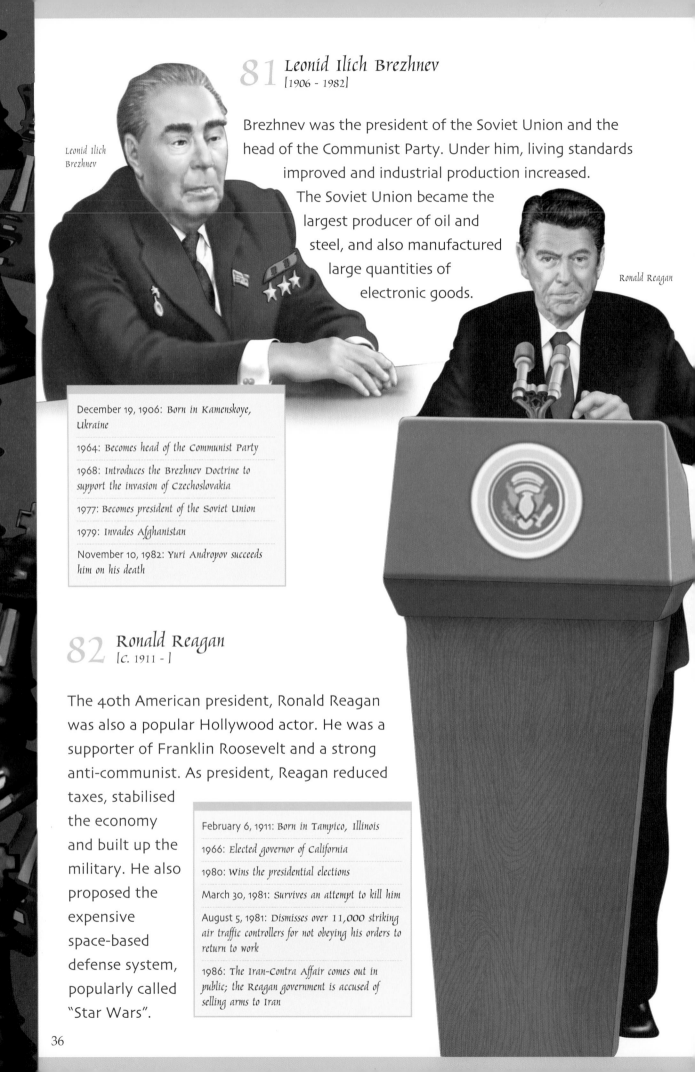

81 Leonid Ilich Brezhnev
[1906 - 1982]

Leonid Ilich Brezhnev

Brezhnev was the president of the Soviet Union and the head of the Communist Party. Under him, living standards improved and industrial production increased. The Soviet Union became the largest producer of oil and steel, and also manufactured large quantities of electronic goods.

Ronald Reagan

December 19, 1906: Born in Kamenskoye, Ukraine

1964: Becomes head of the Communist Party

1968: Introduces the Brezhnev Doctrine to support the invasion of Czechoslovakia

1977: Becomes president of the Soviet Union

1979: Invades Afghanistan

November 10, 1982: Yuri Andropov succeeds him on his death

82 Ronald Reagan
[c. 1911 -]

The 40th American president, Ronald Reagan was also a popular Hollywood actor. He was a supporter of Franklin Roosevelt and a strong anti-communist. As president, Reagan reduced taxes, stabilised the economy and built up the military. He also proposed the expensive space-based defense system, popularly called "Star Wars".

February 6, 1911: Born in Tampico, Illinois

1966: Elected governor of California

1980: Wins the presidential elections

March 30, 1981: Survives an attempt to kill him

August 5, 1981: Dismisses over 11,000 striking air traffic controllers for not obeying his orders to return to work

1986: The Iran-Contra Affair comes out in public; the Reagan government is accused of selling arms to Iran

83 *Sirimavo Bandaranaike*
[c. 1916 - 2000]

1916: Born Sirimavo Ratwatte

1959: Succeeds her husband as prime minister of Ceylon

1972: Promotes the new Constitution and changes the name of the country to Sri Lanka

1977: Her party is defeated in elections

1980: Expelled from the parliament

1988: Loses presidential elections

1994: Returns as prime minister

2000: Dies in Colombo, Sri Lanka

Sirimavo Bandaranaike was the world's first woman prime minister. She succeeded her husband as the prime minister of Ceylon (now Sri Lanka) after he was killed in 1959. During her term, she promoted a new Constitution that declared the country a republic. She lost power in 1977, but returned as prime minister when her daughter, Chandrika Kumaratunga, became president in 1994. Six years later she resigned due to ill health.

84 *John F. Kennedy*
[1917 - 1963]

One of the most popular presidents in American history, JFK's 1,000 days in office were marked by the increase of U.S. role in the space race and by the Vietnam War. His term also saw the Cuban missile crisis and the Bay of Pigs invasion of Cuba. These events worsened the Cold War with the Soviet Union. He also cut taxes and extended federal aid to education and medical care for the aged under Social Security.

John F. Kennedy

May 29, 1917: Born in Brookline, Massachusetts

1953: Marries Jacqueline Lee Bouvier

1956: Writes *Profiles in Courage*, for which he later won the Pulitzer Prize

1961: Becomes the 35th President of the United States; establishes the Alliance for Progress to provide financial aid to the Latin American countries

April 1961: Approves the Bay of Pigs invasion of Cuba by Cuban exiles trained by the Central Intelligence Agency

October 1963: Active involvement in the Vietnam War

November 22, 1963: Shot and killed in Dallas, Texas, by Lee Harvey Oswald

85 *Nelson Mandela*
[1918 -]

July 18, 1918: Born in Qunu, Transkei

1952: Becomes the deputy national president of the African National Congress (ANC)

1960: Launches guerilla warfare against the government

1964: Sentenced to life in prison on charges of sabotage

1990: President Frederik Willem de Klerk releases him

July 1991: Elected president of ANC

1993: Shares Nobel Peace Prize with de Klerk

1994: Becomes president of South Africa after winning first multiracial elections

Nelson Mandela was the first black president of South Africa. He helped to end apartheid in his country. Initially, he conducted his fight in a non-violent manner. However, after a group of peaceful demonstrators were killed in Sharpeville, he declared war on the government. Mandela was sentenced to life imprisonment in 1964, though he continued to inspire the fight against apartheid. Finally, in 1990, President de Klerk released Mandela, who went on to win the first multiracial elections in South Africa.

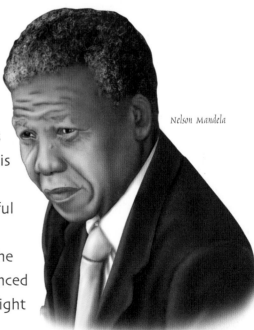

Nelson Mandela

86 Yitzhak Rabin
[1922 - 1995]

Rabin was the prime minister of Israel. He is famous for ordering "Operation Entebbe", in which the Israel Defense Forces rescued passengers of a hijacked plane. He also played a major role in the 1993 Oslo Peace Accords, which created the Palestinian Authority and gave it partial control over parts of Gaza Strip and the West Bank. The accord won Rabin the 1994 Nobel Peace Prize, which he shared with Yasser Arafat and Shimon Peres.

Jimmy Carter

March 1, 1922: Born in Jerusalem

1968: Becomes ambassador to the U.S.

1974: Succeeds Golda Meir as the prime minister of Israel

July 3, 1976: Orders Operation Entebbe

1993: Signs the Oslo Peace Accords with Palestine Liberation Organization (PLO)

1994: Signs peace treaty with Jordan

November 5, 1995: Killed by Yigal Amir, an Israeli law student and activist, in Tel Aviv-Yafo, Israel

87 Jimmy Carter
[1924 -]

Jimmy Carter is one of three American presidents to be awarded the Nobel Peace Prize. While in office, he faced his toughest challenge when 52 Americans were taken hostage by Iranian terrorists. Although the rescue attempt failed, he managed to negotiate their release. Carter is also renowned for his service to society after retirement, and was conferred with the Nobel Peace Prize in 2002.

October 1, 1924: Born in Plains, Georgia

1977: Becomes the 39th U.S. president

September 7, 1977: Turns control of Panama Canal over to Panama

1979: Allows ousted Iranian leader Mohammad Reza Shah Pahlavi into the country, leading to the hostage crisis in Iran

1980: Boycotts the Summer Olympics in Moscow, following Soviet invasion of Afghanistan

May 12, 2002: First American president to visit Cuba during Fidel Castro's rule

2002: Wins the Nobel Peace Prize

88 Margaret Thatcher
[1925 -]

Margaret Thatcher

The first woman prime minister of Britain, she is popularly also called the "Iron Lady". The only British prime minister of the 20th century to serve in three consecutive terms, Margaret Thatcher is both admired and hated for her economic reforms. She strongly supported handing over of national industries to private companies. Differences within her party over political and economic issues eventually forced her to resign.

October 13, 1925: Born in Grantham, Lincolnshire, England

May 4, 1979: Becomes prime minister

1983: Gets re-elected as prime minister

1986: Allows the United States to bomb Libya from air bases in Britain

November 22, 1990: Resigns from office

89 *Kim Dae Jung*
[1925 -]

January 6, 1924: *Born in Hayi-do, Korea*

1997: *Becomes the president of South Korea*

June 2000: *Meets Kim Jong II; wins the Nobel Peace Prize for his efforts to make peace with North Korea*

Kim Dae Jung became the president of South Korea in 1997. He immediately began efforts to befriend North Korea and promote democracy and human rights. In 2000 he travelled to North Korea for a historic meeting with its leader, Kim Jong II. In the same year, Kim Dae Jung was awarded the Nobel Peace Prize for his efforts. However, implications that he might have bribed Kim Jong II for the meeting have harmed his reputation.

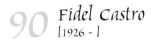

Kim Dae Jung

Fidel Castro

90 *Fidel Castro*
[1926 -]

August 13, 1926: *Born in Holguin Province, Cuba*

January 1, 1959: *Overthrows the Batista government and takes over Havana*

1960: *Signs agreement to buy oil from the Soviet Union*

1961: *Declares Cuba a Communist state; America sponsors the Bay of Pigs invasion*

1962: *Cuban missile crisis occurs after he allows the Soviet Union to place nuclear weapons in Cuba*

President Fidel Castro of the Cuban Republic is credited with improving health facilities and living conditions of the poor, and also with promoting education. His problems with the United States started when he seized the property of big American companies in Cuba, and began to trade with the Soviet Union. Cuba faced major financial problems when the Soviet Union collapsed. Castro then began to encourage foreign companies to come to Cuba. He continues to be a symbol of social justice and progress in his country.

91 Che Guevara
[1928 - 1967]

Che Guevara was a Cuban revolutionary who also served in Fidel Castro's government. Apart from helping Castro to overthrow the Cuban dictator Batista, Guevara was also responsible for cutting ties with the United States and directing Cuba towards the Soviet Union. He left Cuba in 1965 to support freedom struggles in Congo and, subsequently, Bolivia. During a guerilla attack in Bolivia, he was captured and killed by government troops.

92 Henry Kissinger
[1923 -]

Henry Kissinger

As U.S. foreign-policy adviser, Kissinger accomplished several important tasks. He helped begin the Strategic Arms Limitation Talks (SALT) with the Soviet Union to control the production of nuclear weapons.

He also arranged President Nixon's visit to China in 1972. He supported the withdrawal of U.S. troops from Vietnam and later won the Nobel Peace Prize for negotiating the end of fighting with North Vietnam.

93 Yasser Arafat
[1929 -]

Leader of the Palestine Liberation Organization (PLO), Arafat is known for his efforts to maintain peace between Israel and Palestine. Under him, the PLO not only gave up terrorism, but also signed a peace agreement with Israel, for which he won the 1994 Nobel Peace Prize. However, the peace process has not been smooth and terrorist activities still continue.

Yasser Arafat

94 Helmut Kohl
[1930 -]

Helmut Kohl was the chancellor of West Germany and, later, of re-unified Germany as well. Under him, West Germany prospered and became a major power in the world. He launched his efforts to re-unify East and West Germany in 1989, when East Germany began to collapse. Shortly after the fall of the Berlin Wall, Kohl become the first chancellor of a unified Germany.

Helmut Kohl

April 3, 1930: Born in Ludwigshafen am Rhein
1973: Becomes chairman of the Christian Democratic Union
October 1, 1982: Becomes chancellor of West Germany
November 9, 1989: The Berlin Wall falls
December 1990: Becomes chancellor of re-unified Germany
1998: Loses the elections to the Social Democrats led by Gerhard Schroder

Mikhail Gorbachev

95 Mikhail Gorbachev
[1931 -]

Former president of the Soviet Union, Gorbachev is famous for his social and economic reforms – among them, glasnost (openness) and perestroika (economic restructuring). He also ended the Cold War, for which he won the Nobel Peace Prize. In 1988 he allowed Soviet bloc nations like Czechoslovakia to return to democracy. This led to the collapse of Communism in Eastern Europe and resulted in the ultimate break-up of the Soviet Union.

March 2, 1931: Born in Privolye, Stavropol region, Russia
March 11, 1985: Takes over the leadership of the Soviet Union on the death of Konstantin Chernenko
February 1986: Launches glasnost and perestroika
1990: Wins the Nobel Peace Prize for his contribution towards ending the Cold War
1991: Attempt to overthrow him fails; returns to power after spending three days under house arrest, only to find Yeltsin in command
December 25, 1991: Resigns as president
December 26, 1991: The Supreme Soviet officially dissolves the Soviet Union

96 Desmond Tutu
[1931 -]

Tutu was a South African religious leader who fought against apartheid (racial discrimination). He was also the first black Anglican archbishop of Cape Town, South Africa. Winner of the 1984 Nobel Peace Prize, Tutu headed the Truth and Reconciliation Commission that looked into the abuse of human rights during the apartheid era.

1931: Born in Klerksdorp Transvaal

1975: Becomes the first black dean of St. Mary's Cathedral, Johannesburg

1978: Becomes the first black general secretary of the South African Council of Churches

October 16, 1984: Awarded the Nobel Prize for Peace for his contribution to the fight against apartheid

September 7, 1986: Elected archbishop of Cape Town

1996-2003: Heads the Truth and Reconciliation Commission

Desmond Tutu

97 King Hussein
[1935 - 1999]

King Hussein

Hailed as a peacemaker, King Hussein of Jordan was known for his pro-Western stand. This was however, resented by the other Arab nations, especially the Palestinians. Hussein's relations with Palestine worsened when Israel captured the West Bank (earlier a Palestinian territory) during the Arab-Israeli War. Later, though, he played a major role in encouraging peace talks between the Arabs and the Israelis. In 1994, he signed a peace treaty with Israel.

November 14, 1935: Born to Prince Talal of Jordan

1953: Becomes king of Jordan after his grandfather, King Abdullah I, is killed

1967: Loses West Bank to Israel in the Arab-Israeli War

1970: Civil war begins in Jordan

1991: Refuses to join anti-Iraqi forces during the Gulf War

February 7, 1999: Dies in Amman, Jordan

98 F.W. *de Klerk*
[1936 -]

March 18, 1936: *Born in Johannesburg*

1989: *Takes over as president after P.W. Botha resigns*

1990: *Releases Nelson Mandela from prison*

1991: *Calls for drafting a new constitution, leading to the formation of the first multiracial government in South Africa*

1994: *Becomes the vice-president under Mandela's presidency*

1997: *Retires from politics*

As president of South Africa, de Klerk played a big role in ending apartheid in the country. Soon after coming to power, he lifted the ban on anti-racist parties and released Nelson Mandela from prison. In 1991 he abolished all the remaining apartheid laws and set in motion the process for the first multiracial government in South Africa. He received the 1993 Nobel Peace Prize along with Mandela.

99 *John Hume*
[1937 -]

January 18, 1937: *Born in Londonderry, Northern Ireland*

1969: *Becomes a member of parliament*

1979: *Succeeds Gerry Fitt as the leader of the SDLP*

1983: *Becomes a member of parliament of Britain*

1999: *Wins the Nobel Peace Prize*

One of the most important political figures of Northern Ireland, Hume was the founder-member of the Credit Union Party (later the Social Democratic and Labour Party, or SDLP) and a member of the Northern Ireland parliament. He was awarded the 1999 Nobel Peace Prize with David Trimble, the Ulster Unionist party leader, for their efforts to find a peaceful solution to the Northern Ireland conflict.

Oscar Sanchez Arias

John Hume

100 *Oscar Sanchez Arias*
[1941 -]

President of Costa Rica, Arias won the Nobel Peace Prize in 1987. After becoming the president, he worked arduously to bring back peace to Central America, which had been ravaged by civil war. In 1987, he led efforts that called for the end of fighting, the release of political prisoners, and holding of free and fair elections.

1941: *Born in Costa Rica*

1970: *Becomes financial adviser to the president*

1972: *Becomes minister of planning*

1986: *Becomes president of Costa Rica*

1987: *Wins the Nobel Peace Prize for his efforts to maintain peace in Central America*

Glossary

Battle of Kadesh: The battle in which Ramses II is said to have defeated the Hittites, rulers of Asia Minor and Mesopotamia.

Moses: A character from the Bible who received the Ten Commandments from God.

Median rulers: Rulers of the ancient country of Media, situated in present-day north-western Iran.

Lydia: Ancient land, now situated in Turkey.

Babylon: Ancient Middle Eastern city located near the modern city of Al-Hillah, Iraq.

Parthenon: The chief temple of Athena that Ictinus and Callicrates built on the Acropolis at Athens.

Peloponnesian War: War fought between the ancient Greek cities of Athens and Sparta that destroyed Athens.

Plague: A fatal disease that is spread through rats.

King Phillip of Macedon: Eighteenth King of Macedonia (located in south-eastern Europe) and Father of Alexander the Great.

Battle of Issus: Fought between Alexander the Great and Darius III on the Issus plain near the Gulf of Iskenderun (now in southern Turkey).

Battle of Pharsalus: The last battle in the Roman Civil War fought between Julius Caesar and Pompey the Great.

King Ptolemy: Ptolemy XIII, King of Egypt and Cleopatra's brother.

Dictator: An absolute ruler, who uses force to suppress his opponents.

Roman Senate: Governing body of the Roman Republic and the Roman Empire.

Pompey's Theatre: The place where the Roman senate held its meetings.

Roman calendar: It was created in 738 BC by Romulus, the founder of Rome and consisted of only ten months.

Marcus Aemilius Lepidus: Roman leader who controlled parts of Gaul, Spain and Africa after Julius Ceasar's death.

Naval battle: Battle fought at sea

Nervan-Antonine dynasty: Founded by Emperor Nerva, the dynasty ended with Commodus, the son of Marcus Aurelius.

Five Good Emperors: Emperors belonging to the Nervan-Antonine dynasty who helped in the progress of Rome. The five included Nerva, Trajan, Hadrian, Antoninus Pius and Marcus Aurelius.

Suppress: To put an end to something (like a revolt) forcibly.

Uprising: To raise voice against a government or a ruler.

Visigoths: A German tribe that invaded the Roman Empire.

Rua: The first ruler of the unified groups of Huns.

Aetius: Roman Emperor who defeated Attila and his army of Huns at the Battle of Chalons.

Nika Riots: Members and fans of two major chariot racing teams revolted against the Byzantine Emperor Justinian I, demanding the release of those members who had been arrested for murder. They entered the prison and set fire to parts of Constantinople crying out nika, the racing cheer meaning victory.

Lombards: A tribe from north-western Germany that ruled parts of northern Italy until Charlemagne captured the region in 773.

Khusro II: Son of Hormizd IV and grandson of Khusro I, who became the King of Persia with the help of Emperor Maurice I.

Phocas: Officer in the Roman Army, who killed Emperor Maurice to seize power.

Carolingian dynasty: Family of Frankish kings that ruled most of Western Europe from 751-987 AD.

Franks: A group of German tribes settled along the lower and middle Rhine.

Cathedral at Aachen: The oldest cathedral in northern Europe. Charlemagne began its construction in 786.

Baron: A nobleman or a lord.

Capetian dynasty: Founded by Hugh Capet, this dynasty ruled France after the Carolingian kings.

Mongol: Tribes from the Asian country of Mongolia located between Russia and China.

Genghis Khan: Founder and ruler of the Mongol Empire.

Ottoman Empire: Founded by Osman I, a Turkish tribal prince, the empire is named after him. It included Turkey, part of Middle East and North Africa and south-eastern Europe.

Tver: A city in east-central Europe founded in 1246.

Novgorod: An ancient city in north-western Russia.

Tatars: People of Turkish and Mongol origins who invaded Europe six centuries ago.

Muscovy: A state of Russia between the 14th and 18th centuries.

Christopher Columbus: A famous explorer who discovered America.

Holy Roman Emperor: The ruler of modern Germany then called the Holy Roman Empire.

Holy League: An association of Roman Catholics during the French Wars of Religion.

Italian Wars: Series of wars (from 1494-1559) fought by France and Spain, for control over Italy.

Roman Catholicism: Refers to the Roman Catholic Church. The members of this church accept the Pope's (Bishop of Rome) authority in matters of faith.

Protestants: Those who follow Christian religious groups that broke away from the Roman Catholic Church.

Peace of Cateau – Cambresis: Agreement ending the 65-year struggle between France and Spain for the control of Italy.

Tudors: The Tudor dynasty ruled England from 1485-1603. It started with Henry VII and ended with Elizabeth I.

Excommunicate: To bar from a church or a religious community.

Bourbon Kings: Rulers of France, Spain, Naples and Sicily and the descendants of Louis I duc de bourbon.

Navarre: A kingdom, split between France and Spain in the 16th century.

Fanatic: A person obsessed with a cause particularly one that is religious in nature.

Lord Protector: Title used by the acting ruler of England during a brief period of republic or "Commonwealth" in Britain.

Parliament: The governing body of various countries like UK consisting of two houses. (House of Lords and House of Commons).

Navigation Act: Series of laws passed in 1651 that restricted foreign shipping, allowing only English ships to carry goods in and out of Europe.

Dutch Wars: Four wars fought on the sea between England and Netherlands in the 17th and 18th century.

French Revolution: The period between 1789 and 1799 in which Louis XVI, the King of France was overthrown by the people.

Czar: Also spelt Tsar, it is the title given to the Russian or Byzantine emperor. The title is derived from caesar

American Revolution: Also called the American Revolutionary War or American War of Independence, it freed 13 North American colonies of Britain, to form the United States of America.

Treaty of Paris: It ended the American Revolutionary War with the Kingdom of Great Britain and established the United States of America (USA).

Coalition: An alliance of political parties, nations or people.

Alien and Sedition Acts: The laws allowed the American President to drive out any foreigner considered dangerous and made the publishing of nasty articles against the government, a crime.

White House: The U.S. President's house in Washington D.C.

Democratic Party: One of the two major political parties in the U.S. founded by Thomas Jefferson. It was called 'Democratic Republicans' and supported minorities and labourers.

Lewis-Clarke Expedition: An expedition, headed by Captain Meriwether Lewis and William Clark to explore the possibilities of expanding the U.S. boundary.

Indian Removal Act: It offered the American Indian tribes, unsettled land in the west in exchange for their lands inside the state borders.

Exile: To be banished from one's land

Gran Colombia: Also called Greater Colombia, it consisted of modern Colombia, Venezuela, Ecuador and Panama.

Emancipation Proclamation: Law issued to free slaves in the Southern states of America.

American civil war: War between the U.S. Federal government (Union) and 11 Southern states that fought to break away from the union.

Gettysburg Address: Speech made by President Abraham Lincoln at the dedication of a cemetery at Gettysburg, Pennsylvania, for those killed at the Battle of Gettysburg during the American Civil War.

Underground Railroad: A group of secret routes consisting of safe houses and other facilities owned by those against slavery. Slaves were rescued and helped to escape the United States to places like Canada that offered them protection.

League of Nations: Organisation, like the United Nations, created to promote international peace. It was established by the Allies at the end of World War I.

Disarmament: Reduction of a country's military forces and weapons.

Treaty of Versailles: Agreement ending World War I signed at the Palace of Versailles.

Geneva Protocol: A treaty created by the League of Nations for peaceful settlement of disagreements between nations.

Locarno Pact: An agreement signed between Germany and the Allied powers that determined the borders and normalised relations between the two parties.

Irish Free State: The state comprising 26 of the 32 counties of Ireland separated from the United Kingdom under the Anglo-Irish treaty.

Ambassador: A government official sent as a representative of one country to another.

North Atlantic Treaty Organisation: An international organisation that protects its member nations from military attacks.

Korean War: Fought between South and North Korea (1950-53) over division of territories.

Four Freedoms Speech: Franklin D Roosevelt's speech about the freedom of speech, religion, freedom from want and from fear of physical aggression.

Easter Rising: Attempt by Irish Republicans to forcibly free Ireland from Britain.

Fascism: Dictatorship. Rule using military force.

Free French forces: French movement to continue war against Germany after France's 1940 defeat in World War II.

Pathan: A native of Afghanistan.

Cold War: Open but weapon-less enmity between the U.S and the U.S.S.R and their allies.

Hungarian revolution: Popular uprising to free Hungary from Soviet control.

Yuri Gagarin: First person to travel into space.

Sputnik I: World's first artificial satellite put into orbit on October 1957.

Brezhnev Doctrine: A policy that defended Soviet involvement in countries like Czechoslovakia that were its military allies.

Vietnam War: Attempt by U.S. backed South Vietnam to prevent the unification of North and South Vietnam under communist leadership.

Bay of Pigs invasion: Unsuccessful attempt by 1500 Cuban exiles opposed to Fidel Castro to invade Cuba. It was supported by the United States.

Palestinian Authority: Also called the Palestinian National Authority, it is the governing body of the Palestinian regions of the West Bank and Gaza Strip.

Palestine Liberation Organization: Political organisation formed in 1964 to fight for a Palestinian State.

Berlin Wall: The wall surrounding West Berlin built after 2.5 million East Germans fled to West Germany between 1949 and 1961. It was erected on the night of August 12, 1961.

Glasnost: Russian for openness, it allowed open criticism of the government and encouraged public discussion of political and social issues.

Perestroika: Russian word meaning restructuring, it reduced the Communist government's involvement in the country's governance and economy.

Soviet bloc nations: Communist countries of the time like Czechoslovakia, Romania, and Hungary, which had political and military ties with the U.S.S.R.